WHAT OTHERS ARE SAYING ABOUT THIS BOOK

"These thoughts will touch the heart of the caregiver and inspire a deeper commitment to authentic service."

—Ragna Rostad, R.N., Certified
AIDS Counselor

"This book is a source of renewed hope in times of despair and a celebration of the joys of success."

—Cecelia M. Holland, R.N., Chief,
Nursing Services, VA Medical
Center, Fort Harrison, MT

"*Inspirations for Caregivers* nurtures that often neglected place within all caregivers that can only be tended by the heart. This book should be at each nursing station in every hospital."

—Cindy Mikluscak-Cooper, author of
*Living In Hope: A 12-Step Approach
for Persons at Risk or Infected with HIV*

"*Inspirations for Caregivers* not only praises the work of the caregiver, but also deeply questions the motives behind our many deeds of service. An excellent self-assessment tool!"

—Dr. Phillip Kavanaugh, author of
Magnificent Addictions

"Help for caregivers is so much needed. I believe that loving and nurturing the self is especially important for caregivers. If we deplete our energies, we cannot give in the loving way we would want to."

—Louise Hay, author of *You Can
Heal Your Life*

"Being a novice caregiver, I always wondered if I was doing everything right. After reading Caryn's book I realized that if you come from the heart, you'll give your patient all he really wants—compassion and love."

—Joan Lucas, caregiver of elderly father

"This book is a compelling collection of years of wisdom in human service."

—Candace Snow & David Willard, authors of *I'm Dying to Take Care of You*

"This book reflects the diverse emotions we feel as helping professionals—from laughter to tears. As a bereaved parent and a professional counselor, I highly recommend it."

—William Young, certified rehabilitation counselor and leader of the Independent Living Movement

"These writings carry the seeds of inspiration that can soothe a yearning soul."

—Jacquelyn Small, author of *Awakening in Time* and *Transformers*

"Every page of this little book offers a gentle reminder of who we really are and what we are really trying to do in helping others, professionally or personally. We all need such reminders to truly by of service to a world that needs the best each of us has to give."

—Molly Young Brown, author of *Growing Whole: Self Realization on an Endangered Planet* and *The Unfolding Self: Psychosynthesis and Counseling*

DEDICATION

To my granddaughter Cedella, and to her parents who have given to her so selflessly: McKell Eldredge and Jonathan Ward.

And to my son, Cody Eldredge, and to Roya Marashi

And to my loving partner, Douglas York

Commune-A-Key Publishing
P O Box 507
Mount Shasta CA 96067
U.S.A.

(Library of Congress Cataloging in-Publication Data)

Summers, Caryn L (Caryn Lea)
    Inspirations for caregivers / by Caryn Summers
    p. cm.
    Includes bibliographical references and index.
    Preassigned LCCN: 93-071074
    ISBN 1-881394-08-5

    1. Care of the sick—Meditations. 2. Medical personnel—
Meditations. 3. Caregivers—Meditations. I.Title.
R725.55.S85 1993   610.19
                                         QB193-574

Cover design by Gaelyn & Bram Larrick,
Lightbourne Images, Kelseyville, CA.
Printed by Griffin Press, Sacramento CA.

ISBN 1-881394-08-5 $8.95 softcover

Inspirations for Caregivers

Edited By:
Caryn Lea Summers, R.N.

ACKNOWLEDGMENTS

I want to thank the Caregivers who reviewed these quotes:
James Parker, M.D.
Ellen Cleaver, MFCC
Wendy Crist, RN
Ragna Rostad, RN
William Young, Counseling Psychologist
Joan Lucas, Caregiver to her 96 year old father

Thanks to my nurse support group that gently reminds me
of the meaning of service and unconditional love.

Special thanks to Douglas York, my partner who has supported my
vision for Commune-A-Key, and who cared for me during the
stressful hours of writing books and starting new businesses.

I am also grateful to my friend and business associate,
Ragna Rostad, who shares the vision of service to our helpers.

I want to thank my friends and graphic design artists,
Gaelyn and Bram Larrick of Lightbourne Images, for their
unique gifts of artistic expression and organization.

And I give deepest appreciation to my first Caregivers:
my parents Carole and Charles Summers. I love you.

INTRODUCTION

While writing my second book, *Caregiver, Caretaker,* I learned about the pitfalls of caring for other people before caring for ourselves. I found the potential for an addiction to giving too much among caregivers. Questions arose: "Why do we keep giving? What are the motivations that keeps us in the helping profession? How can we keep the passion for caring alive, that beautiful drive to give that is required of us as caregivers? How can we keep a balanced perspective on caring?

I identified the negative roles that we caregivers often find ourselves playing: martyr, victim, rescuer, fixer, critic, saint. Now I desired a positive view of caregiving that would provide me with faith in helping, and would give my chosen profession the dignity that it deserves.

The concept of "caregiver" is complex. Some of the quotes in this book almost glorify the role of caregiving, where others deeply question the motives behind caring. Some of the opinions expound unselfish, "Christ-like" giving. Others call this behavior a character defect that is based on the need to be needed. The many interpretations of the word, "serve" are equally interesting. To some, the word carries a negative connotation, as a job description for a servant, or a as a prison sentence. To others the word "serve" conveys the deepest spiritual experience.

Different divisions of the helping professions — nurse, physician, therapist, attendant, family member of a homebound person — bring with them differing perspectives. The people in these divisions each share their portion of the truth, and provide us with a composite meaning of "Caregiver."

The meaning of caregiving will remain unique for each individual. As Ram Dass states so beautifully in the final analysis, "Caring is a reflex. Someone slips, your arm goes out... You live, you help." It may be as simple as that.

Caring is a reflex. Someone slips, your arm goes out. A car is in a ditch, you join the others and push. A colleague at work has the blues, you let her know you care. It all seems natural and appropriate. You live, you help.

— Ram Dass

Rather than being afraid of tears, look at them as a chance to break through the isolation and finally connect with your loved one. If tears begin to well up in your eyes, let them come. They will communicate to your family member or friend that you care deeply. Your tears will also give permission to your loved one that he or she can cry as well without feeling uneasy.

— Leonard Felder, Ph.D.

The way of the heart is one of compassion and emotional perception. Therefore, it is never appropriate to suppress an emotion, or to disregard what you feel.

— Gary Zukav

*S*elf-care cannot be accom-
plished without self-love. We
need to ask if we feel worthy
enough to care for ourselves, even
as a priority over caring for others.

—Caryn Summers, R.N.

If you have never loved yourself, never really loved yourself, gently and unconditionally, now is the time to do that. Love yourself, forgive yourself, and at the same time, know that there is nothing to forgive. Love other people, and let them love you. You'll never be bored. Unconditional love can do some amazing things, and it's a real safety net. And we can do amazing things when we know that we are safe. Miracles happen every day.

— Max Navarre

I must be genuine in caring for the other. I must "ring true." There must not be a significant gap between how I act and what I really feel, between what I say and what I feel.

—Milton Mayeroff

Caring is the essence of nursing — caring for, caring with, and caring about. No one, however, through pen or canvas, will ever be able to entirely capture the true art and the caring spirit of nursing. Both defy expression!

— M. Patricia Donahue, RN.

What an experience having cancer is. My whole life will be different for it as long as I live, and, yes, I am one of those who wants to live to be a hundred. An exceptional nurse at the hospital told me to 'live each day to the max.' Do you know what the max turned out to be once I was up and around again after two surgeries in five weeks' time? It was hanging up laundry in the sun with a cat rubbing against my leg.

— patient with ovarian cancer
in a self-created remission.

If we doctors would admit our mortality, then we would find a way to succeed with even the sickest of our patients, sometimes simply holding their hands when they are frightened and in pain, other times helping them understand the meaning of their illness and how they can use it to experience life and love. It is my patients, out of their kindness and their wisdom, who have taught me this, and it seems to me that whenever I am in danger of forgetting it, another patient helps me return to that knowledge.

— Bernie Siegel, M.D.

Placing service in a spiritual perspective in no way diminishes what we have to offer others through training, experience, individuality, special skills, or sense of humor. Quite the reverse. Our particular talents and unique qualities are likely to come forth more reliably when we do have a richer and more spacious sense of who we are — the very promise of all spiritual practice.

— Ram Dass

would like to see healing help create a world where it's safe for all of us to love each other. That would take care of many problems. To create this world, we each have to live it ourselves. And J think it's the therapists' obligation to do what they can to help themselves.

— Louise L. Hay

You can exchange all suffering for joy this very day. Practice in earnest, and the gift is yours.

— From A Course in Miracles.

To me, healing is releasing from the past. It is retraining my mind so as not to see the shadow of the past on anyone. It is learning not to make interpretations of people's behavior or motives. It is letting go of the desire to want to change another person. It is letting go of expectations, assumptions, and the desire to control or manipulate another person.

— Gerald Jampolsky, M.D.

The experience of burnout has a particular kind of poignance. Having started out to help others, we're somehow getting wounded ourselves. What we had in mind was expressing compassion. Instead, what we seem to be adding to the universe is more suffering — our own — while we're supposedly helping.

— Ram Dass

The woundedness in each of us connects us in trust. My woundedness evokes your healer, and your woundedness evokes my healer. Then the two healers can collaborate together.

— Rachel Naomi Remen, M.D.

*C*odependence draws us off balance into caring for others at the expense of ourselves, creating professional disillusionment and personal pain — anything but an inspiring practice.

— Candace Snow and
David Willard, R.N.

One of the major occupational hazards of the healing arts is an overidentification with the ability to heal. Therapists need to keep in mind that their healing ability consists mainly of a gift for influencing, stimulating, and inspiring clients to move along the course of their own healing path; and sometimes nothing the therapist does will work.

— Martin Rossman, M.D.

I wouldn't miss life
for anything!

— Anne Wilson Schaef

For me, there is a reverence for life. It means enjoying the sunshine, the rain, a dust storm, walking down the city street, and looking to see the pleasure, to smell the fresh air. It means bringing the country with me to the city. It's working hard in my garden. It's reading a good book. It's being with people I enjoy. It's even being with people I don't enjoy. It's learning to choose. It's learning I can't care for everyone. It's having an obligation not to cause pain in this life and to ease it when I can.

— Nola, Nurse and Nurse Educator

The problem for many family members and friends of people with a long-term illness is that they are usually too busy to slow down and unravel their feelings. They might be afraid of falling apart if they let go of the flood of emotions they've been holding inside.

Is there a safe and manageable way to release some of the emotional pain you've been carrying ever since your loved one became ill or disabled?

— Leonard Felder, Ph.D.

That evening I went to the lounge. It was homey. The head nurse could see me with tears running down my face. She asked, "Do you need to talk?" and I said, "Yeah, I need to know more about leukemia." I wanted to know what it was, how it worked, what happens with it. The thing that impressed me was that I could feel her pain for me. I cried for a while. For the first time through all this, I cried in front of someone else.

— Val, Wife of a Patient

Wounding is the traditional training ground for the healer. Those who have, through accident or illness, vividly confronted the reality of their own death often return to life with a renewed sense of wonder and strength.

— Dr. Jean Houston

Those who do not know how to weep with their whole heart don't know how to laugh either.

— Golda Meir

One thing I say to therapists is if you can't stomach it, don't do it. If you have to lie to yourself that things aren't as they are, don't do it because there's no reason to make yourself sick. I have found that if a person is in front of me, they have strength because they're living and therefore I work with the strength.

— Virginia Satir

Without consistently con-
fronting and questioning our
own skewed thoughts and feelings,
there is little integrity and much
inauthenticity in our work with others. Patients know when our words
don't match our behavior; so do our
colleagues. When we say to them,
'Have hope,' 'Try,' and at the same
time model our own hopelessness
about our compulsive overeating,
the organization in which we work,
or our relationships, our patients
and colleagues note the lack of
congruence.

— Candace Snow and
David Willard, R.N.

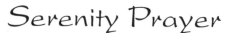

Serenity Prayer

God grant me the Serenity
to accept the things J
cannot change,
Courage to change the things J
can, and
the wisdom to know the difference.

Living one day at a time;
Enjoying one moment at a time;
Accepting hardship as the pathway
to peace.

(cont)

Taking, as He did, this world as
it is, not as I would have it;

Trusting that He will make all things
right if I surrender to His will;

That I may be reasonably happy in
this life,
And supremely happy with Him
forever in the next.

— Reinhold Niebuhr

To me, healing is letting God write the script of my life. It is choosing to let God's will and my will be one.

— Gerald Jampolsky, M.D.

In a true healing relationship, both heal and both are healed.

— Rachel Naomi Remen, M.D.

Gratitude remains incomplete until I have expressed my thanks for what I have received.... I am grateful for living the meaning of my life (for having appropriate others that need me and for being able to care for them) and, more generally, for life itself. I am thankful for the opportunity and the capacity to give of myself. It is because I give that I receive, which, of course, does not mean that I give in order to receive. I cannot be grateful for what I believe another was forced to give me, and the conviction that "it was due me" is equally incompatible with gratitude.

—Milton Mayeroff

I see hope as a daily process of looking for something to feel good about. Every single day I try to find something to be grateful for — maybe that my father is still here with us, that I'm learning more about how to be a better caregiver, or that I can still say "I love you" even if he seems not to be listening.

— Leonard Felder, Ph.D.

All the healing techniques in the world won't really help unless love goes with them.

— Louise L. Hay

If I speak with the tongues of men and of angels, but have not love, I am only a resounding gong or a clanging cymbal. If I have the gift of prophecy and can fathom all mysteries and all knowledge, and if I have a faith that can move mountains, but have not love, I am nothing. If I give all I possess to the poor and surrender my body to the flames, but have not love, I gain nothing.

— 1 Corinthians: 13.

W hat is to give
light must
endure burning.

— Vicktor Frankl

Our most profound growth comes during our most painful times. Becoming aware of the difficulty is the first step in finding the solution. Once we acknowledge our despair and admit that we are powerless, we become empowered. Once we admit that our lives are unmanageable, we no longer have to pretend to be in control. By stating our confusion, we make the first move toward clarity. When denial stops, the process of healing begins. In the center of chaos lies the promise of clarity.

— Caryn Summers, R.N.

The body knows
and the soul
knows: Only our minds
can lie.

— Jacquelyn Small

We labor under the myth that it is the ministrations of health-care providers that cure or heal people. This is simply an illusion, a product of faulty logic. The assumption is that if a patient gets well after surgery, she gets well because of surgery. The reality is that surgery does not cure/heal. Drugs do not cure/heal. Acupuncture, or crystals, or homeopathy do not cure/heal. The person who undergoes the surgery, or takes the drug, or receives the alternative treatment must heal herself. Any or all of the above-named ministrations may be necessary to remove barriers to self-healing or to stimulate it, but they are not sufficient causes for healing.

— Janet F. Quinn, R.N.

Sometimes give your services for nothing, calling to mind a previous benefaction or present satisfaction ... For where there is love of man, there is also love of the art. For some patients, though conscious that their condition is perilous, recover their health simply through their contentment with the goodness of the physician.

— Hippocrates, 460-377 B.C.

Thoughtfulness, the kindly regard for others, is the beginning of holiness.

— Mother Teresa of Calcutta.

I served for many dysfunctional reasons. I served so that you would like me. I became a nurse so that I could look at your problems instead of my own. I served so that I could feel in control. When not in control, I felt an inner anxiety that stemmed from an uncontrollable past. I served so that I could feel needed, since I needed to be needed. I served so that you would give me esteem, because I could not give myself any.

—Caryn Summers, R.N.

The reason you cannot
earn your worth is
because you are already
worthy. All you can do is
accept what is already yours.

— Carmen Renee Berry

*C*all the world, if you
please, The veil
of Soulmaking.
Then you will find out
The use of the world...

— John Keats

When you meet anyone,
remember it is a
holy encounter.
As you see him you will see
yourself.
As you treat him you will treat
yourself.
As you think of him you will think of
yourself.
Never forget this,
for in him you will find yourself or
lose yourself.

— From A Course in Miracles.

43

I get a massage almost every week, no matter where I am. I eat a healthy diet, I schedule time alone, and if I get to a point where I feel I need a block of time and I don't have it, I'll cancel. In general, I really listen to my body and pay attention to my needs.

— Anne Wilson Schaef

L earn to get in touch with silence within yourself and know that everything in this life has a purpose. There are no mistakes, no coincidences. All events are blessings given to us to learn from.

—Elizabeth Kubler-Ross

For all things born in truth
must die,
and out of death in truth
comes life.
Face to face with what
must be,
Cease thou from sorrow.

— Bhagavad-Gita 2:27

No excuse is good enough for neglecting to reach out and embrace our loved ones while they are still alive. Death can come when we least expect it, so we must take every opportunity to give our love to those around us. The time is now!

— Barry and Joyce Vissell

Take two jokes
and call me in
the morning.

— source unknown

Nothing may be more important than being gentle with ourselves. Whether we're professionals working a sixty-hour week or simply family members called upon to care daily for a sick relative, facing suffering continuously is no small task. We learn the value of recognizing our limits, forgiving ourselves our bouts of impatience or guilt, acknowledging our own needs. We see that to have compassion for others we must have compassion for ourselves.

— Ram Dass

We ourselves want to be needed. We do not only have needs, we are also strongly motivated by neededness... We are restless when we are not needed, because we feel "unfinished," "incomplete," and we can only get completed in and through these relationships. We are motivated to search not only for what we lack and need but also for that for which we are needed, what is wanted from us.

— Andras Angyal

*C*odependents don't have rela-tionships — they have caseloads !

— Jann Mitchell

Love incorporates compassion, which means to suffer with another person. Compassion is different from pity, which means to suffer for the other person. When we feel compassion, we can release our expectations and allow others to choose their own path. With compassion, we can love others, even when they err. When we love ourselves and others, forgiveness happens naturally.

— Caryn Summers, R.N.

All I want is for you to sit down here next to me. I don't care about the nurse; the IV is working fine; the bed is comfortable. Just sit with me.

— A Patient

For so much of my life I was run by this nagging voice in the back of my head that kept insisting, "You're not doing enough! You're not doing enough!" But now I'm starting to listen to my body a lot more. It needs tender loving care and I'm the only one who can provide that. Even though I always feared that if I took better care of myself it would mean I'd become selfish or self-indulgent, I've discovered that's not the case.

— Leonard Felder, Ph.D.

We are most
effective as
caregivers when we
are centered in our
own sense of well-
being.

—Caryn Summers, R.N.

Caregiving and rescuing
are a lot different.
Rescuing can make the
rescuer feel good, but it might
not make the patient feel good.

— Dave, a Patient

The curing relationship is not always healthy for the client. While benefiting in some ways by the relationship, the client may also be diminished because it is a dependent relationship. There is not much room for strength or growth in the kind of curing relationship that we're taught in professional schools. We can fix the fixable, but we don't evoke healing, and we don't participate in the healing that may arise naturally. The fixing relationship assumes that healing is not natural. Healing is natural.

— Rachel Naomi Remen, M.D.

The reward, the real grace, of conscious service... is the opportunity not only to help relieve suffering but to grow in wisdom, experience greater unity, and have a good time while we're doing it.

— Ram Dass

One cannot have
wisdom without
living life.

— Dorothy McCall

"As you teach
so will you learn."

If that is true, and it is true
indeed, do not forget that what
you teach is teaching you.

— From *A Course in Miracles.*

My problem is a teacher to me—a vital contact with my past that I am to attend to and make conscious. It has surfaced so I can know it.

— Jacquelyn Small

Laughter is inner jogging:
100 good belly laughs are
the cardiovascular equivalent
of 10 minutes of rowing.

— source unknown

If it's been too long since you were able to laugh, to relax with a friend, to spend quiet moments in a natural setting, or to have someone lovingly prepare a bowl of soup for you, now is your chance to stop being a martyr. Who can you call right now to schedule a few hours replenishing your strength and maybe even having a good time? If the first person you call is unavailable, don't give up. Who is your second choice for someone whose support can help renew your energies? Who is your third choice? Make sure you don't give up until you find someone who can join you in a few hours of sustenance and renewal.

— Leonard Felder, Ph.D.

*B*eyond treating the symptom, the physician has the responsibility of representing wellness to the patient, of being a totem of wellness rather than a figure associated only with disease.

— Dawson Church

J know that peace is not
the absence of war and
that health is not the absence
of illness — it's a whole
other thing.

— Virginia Satir

There is a thin line between giving and unhealthy "enabling" (i.e., supporting someone else's dependency or irresponsibility). Sometimes we persist in giving to people who use our gifts and energy only to help themselves continue in a destructive pattern.

— Carol S. Pearson

You must be careful to do what is appropriate and evolutionary for the other. Otherwise you become a compulsive cornucopia, burying someone under all the gifts you are pouring out. Your apparent generosity is not always appreciated, and indeed may be deeply resented.

— Dr. Jean Houston

The symptoms and the illness are not the same thing. The illness exists long before the symptoms. Rather than being the illness, the symptoms are the beginning of its cure. The fact that they are unwanted makes them all the more a phenomenon of grace — a gift of God, a message from the unconscious, if you will, to initiate self-examination and repair.

— M. Scott Peck, M.D.

The cure is at the
center of the ill.

—Sri Aurobindo

In truth, no one had ever adequately prepared me for the wonders of nursing: the emotional ups and downs; the spiritual element that can tax one's faith, can shake it to its very foundation; the observation of miracles; and the growth and development that occur beyond one's wildest imagination. In the final analysis, nursing puts us in touch with being human.

— M. Patricia Donahue, R.N.

I would have a course called 'Why you Became a Doctor,' so that students can understand what motivated them at both a conscious and an unconscious level to choose the medical profession. This course would help students deal with their feelings as they face up to the fact that some of their patients are going to die, and that they themselves are mortal — which doctors don't like to admit.

— Bernie Siegel, M.D.

We realize that what we are accomplishing is a drop in the ocean. But if this drop were not in the ocean, it would be missed.

— Mother Teresa of Calcutta.

I don't think we can stand back and look at ourselves and our culture and the way we live in the world, raping the world, without feeling sad. I try to see life like a lake. The anger and the politics and the bitching and the back-biting and the stabbing and the conflict are all froth on the surface in a windy storm. The essence of humanizing comes from the deep, dark blue waters underneath. That's where the dolphins and the whales swim. That's where the mysteries are.

— Graeme, Psychologist

Many of us do not allow ourselves to retreat from worldly pressures. We are needed by our children, our mates, our co-workers. We may not know how to say "No, I am not available ... I'm on retreat." The activities of the world tend to cry out louder than our own heart.

— Caryn Summers, R.N.

You must learn to
be still in the
midst of activity and
to be vibrantly alive
in repose.

— Indira Gandhi

I have a friend, a chemotherapy nurse in a children's cancer ward, whose job it is to pry for any available vein in an often emaciated arm to give infusions of chemicals that sometimes last as long as twelve hours and which are often quite discomforting to the child. He is probably the greatest pain giver the children meet in their stay in the hospital. Because he has worked so much with his own pain, his heart is very open. He works with his responsibilities in the hospital as a "laying on of hands with love and acceptance." There is little in him that causes him to withdraw, that reinforces the painfulness of the experience for the children. He is a warm, open space which encourages them to trust whatever they feel. And it is he whom the children most often ask for at the time they are dying. Although he is the main pain-giver, he is also the main love-giver.

— Ram Dass

The beauty of the world has two edges, one of laughter, one of anguish, cutting the heart asunder.

—Virginia Woolf

Pure altruism as a motivation for nursing evolved into the care of the sick or disabled as a corporal work of mercy:

To feed the hungry.
To give water to the thirsty.
To clothe the naked.
To visit the imprisoned.
To shelter the homeless.
To care for the sick.
To bury the dead.

— M. Patricia Donahue, RN.

Most of those who make professional careers in the healing arts start with a burning desire to enrich the lives of others by offering them the gifts of freedom from pain, relief from anxiety and suffering, and the blessings of wellness. Healers are healers because they want to give.

— Dawson Church

Where did our feelings of insecurity first occur? When did we no longer feel protected? When did we first feel loss of control in our lives? When did it become unacceptable to feel our anger? Where did our greatest fears originate? How old were we when we first felt betrayed? When did we stop trusting?

— Caryn Summers, R.N.

First try to discover your own childhood, then take the experience seriously... Try to feel, and help the patient to feel... study the history of childhood... Therapy has to open you as well as the patient for feeling in your life. It has to awaken you from a sleep.

— Alice Miller

One disadvantage of using the word healer is that it can create a misconception; it implies that people should depend upon others to do their healing for them.

— Jack Schwarz

The longer I practice medicine,
the less sure I am of the
dividing line between healer and
those in need of healing. Patients
whose overwhelming physical
problems made me feel useless
have taught me volumes about the
true nature of my calling, thereby
restoring my faith in myself as
a doctor.

— Bernie Siegel, M.D.

One Sunday morning, a night nurse decided to stop by her church on the way home from work. She found it very difficult to stay awake through the sermon and was soon dozing.

At one point, the preacher began pounding the pulpit and shouting "The crucifixion was all your fault! By your sins, you drove in the nails that crucified our Lord!"

The night nurse abruptly awakened, leapt to her feet, and cried, "No, it wasn't my fault! It was 3 to 11 shift!"

— Liz Schultz, RN

Love and guilt
cannot coexist,
and to accept one is to
deny the other.

— From *A Course in Miracles.*

If you and I are participating in the healing process together, it is my woundedness that allows me to connect to you in your woundedness. I know what suffering is. I also know that you may feel separated from other people by your suffering. You may feel lost, frightened, trapped. My woundedness allows me to find you and be with you in a way that is nonjudgmental. You are not the sick one or the weak one. We are here together, both capable of suffering, both capable of healing.

— Rachel Naomi Remen, M.D.

Being Nobody

Have you ever felt like
nobody?
Just a tiny speck of air.
When everyone's around you,
And you are just not there.

— Karen Crawford, Age 9.

The recognition of fallibility comes hard for many modern healers. And, not surprisingly, we physicians expend ingenious efforts to conceal this eternal fact.

— Larry Dossey, M.D.

We must accept our vulnerability and limitations in regard to others. This is essential in gaining their confidence. We cannot expect to help others from the "outside."

— Mother Teresa of Calcutta.

When I was a student nurse, a story was told about one of my classmates who went to get her patient ready for physical therapy. He had just had a stroke and was not much help with the transfer. She had finally gotten him into a sitting position and was about to call for assistance when the doctor came in the room. The MD asked what she was doing. She said that she was getting the patient up for physical therapy. "That's strange" said the doctor. "I was coming in to sign the death certificate."

— Leslie Garfield, RN

How can I keep my heart open and not go under? I've got my own life to live, after all. Still, I'd like to do more for others. What do I have to offer, and what would help most? Complicated business, all this.... Look, you do the best you can...

— Ram Dass

Consider the Buddha, whose father sought to protect his beloved child from the misery of the world. When the son finally escaped from the prison of his father's palace and discovered illness, old age, poverty, and asceticism, he never returned home again. You, too, may have had to leave those who, in the name of love, have held you too tightly in their embrace.

— Dr. Jean Houston

An easy litmus test can determine whether one is giving or enabling. If, when we give, we feel either used or smugly superior, it is time to look at what really is going on. Healthy giving is respectful of both the giver and the receiver.

— Carol S. Pearson

To share often and much ...
to know even one life has
breathed easier
because you have lived.
This is to have succeeded.

— Ralph Waldo Emerson.

Comfort: one simple word. Yet this concept helps to create a world of nursing that encompasses the integration of concern for the spiritual, emotional, and physical aspects of patient care. It is through comfort and comfort measures that nurses provide strength, hope, solace, support, encouragement, and assistance to individuals, groups, and communities as they experience a multitude of life circumstances.

— M. Patricia Donahue, RN.

Healing in the future must involve major shifts in the way we think about health and illness. The focus of a health-care system must be on facilitating wholeness, which means facilitating right relationship. The techniques are beside the point. What must occur is twofold: the revaluing of the feminine principle and its ways, and the empowerment of individuals and communities to create their own health and healing.

— Janet F. Quinn, R.N.

Health is not equivalent to happiness, surfeit, or success. It is foremost a matter of being wholly one with whatever circumstances we find ourselves in. Even our death is a healthy event if we fully embrace the fact of our dying... The issue is awareness, of living in the present. Whatever our present existence consists of, if we are at one with it, we are healthy.

— Elizabeth Kubler-Ross

There are many physicians to whom the fact of their own woundedness is apparent, and they handle this knowledge with a grace that empowers them as healers. Yet others do not. And the unfortunate way that the inner fact of woundedness is too often dealt with is through projecting it onto the external world in an attempt to rid oneself of something painful. Far better that someone else should be wounded, weak, or fallible than I, so the rationalization goes.

— Larry Dossey, M.D.

Without an awareness of our feelings we cannot experience compassion. How can we share the sufferings and the joys of others if we cannot experience our own?

— Gary Zukav

A guru once explained the concept of self-aware-ness and wisdom to his disciple. He slowly drew a circle in the sand and said, "Inside this small circle contains all of the knowledge that you possess." Pointing to the circumference of the circle, he said, "The area surrounding the circle contains how much you do not know." Then quietly drawing a much larger circle around his disciple's small, humble one, he explained, "Inside this larger space contains all of my knowledge." Pointing to the huge surface area that surrounded his own circle he whispered, "This is how much I have yet to learn."

— Caryn Summers, R.N.

The most elusive
knowledge of all
is self-knowledge.

—Mirra Komarovsky

I have a dream — a vision of how caring could be. Of how having been ill wouldn't mean fear and loneliness... Where a whole institution of caring people understood that nothing is as therapeutic as recognizing the emotional pain, not just the physical pain. I have a vision that doctors could talk compassionately. That families could talk openly. That patients could talk freely...

I have a vision that the caregivers would touch patients, gently, caringly and not only physically. That all would recognize that with every touch, every smile, every word, we enter a temple. A temple so sacred, so impressionable, so beautiful that every fingerprint leaves its mark. That with every moment we enter the temple of the self.

(cont.)

I have a vision that caregivers would share a strength — a strength that comes only from a common purpose, that comes from belonging to a community of people who believe that caring makes a difference, that custodians matter as much as physicians, that volunteers have a place beside nurses, that letters and titles matter less than kindness.

That line-ups are no more. That people are cared for before paper. That voices convey caring before directions. That waiting rooms reflect hope rather than convenience. That death means knowing a lot of people care. That there will be no physical pain and no aloneness. That tears could give way to laughter and anger to tenderness. That joy could surface in our sadness.

— Ronna Fay Jevne, PhD.

When experiencing diffi-culty in discerning your own needs, it may be helpful to begin by observing what you provide for others. Often we give to other people what we unconsciously know that we need ourselves.

— Carmen Renee Berry

If I stop to think about it, I help out for all kinds of reasons. Maybe it's because I should; it's a matter or responsibility. But there's usually a maze of other motives: a need for self-esteem, approval, status, power; the desire to feel useful, find intimacy, pay back some debt.

— Ram Dass

*T*hose whom we support hold us up in life.

—Marie Ebner von Eshenbach

At a certain point "helper" and "helped" simply begin to dissolve. What's real is the helping — the process in which we're all blessed, according to our needs and our place at the moment. How much we can get back in giving! How much we can offer in the way we receive!

— Ram Dass

Children fear their shadows
Yet have no need
for fright.
For if there were no shadows
How could we know the light?

— James Dillot Freeman

It was in the darkness that I found the light. It was in the pain that I found the gain. It was in the dying that I found the life. It was in the aloneness that I found the need of prayer. And it is through the love of God that I found meaning in my life.

— Susan, Patient

I can conceive that one day medical schools will emphasize not entirely the known, but a healthy dose of the unknown as well. It might give us not only a true picture of medical science, but also a truer vision of ourselves as well. It might remind us of something we have almost forgotten as modern physicians, and which we desperately need to remember: that first, and finally, and without exception, we are wounded healers.

— Larry Dossey, M.D.

$\mathcal{J}$f $\mathcal{I}$ don't do me,
$\mathcal{I}$ don't get done.

— Jacquelyn Small

*T*hose who are healed become the instruments of healing.

— From *A Course in Miracles*

The Prayer of St. Francis

Lord, make me an instrument of
Thy peace;
Where there is hatred, let me sow love;
Where there is doubt, faith;
Where there is despair, hope;
Where there is darkness, light;
and where there is sadness, joy.

O Divine Master, grant that I may not
so much seek to be consoled, as to
console;
to be understood, as to understand;
to be loved, as to love;
for it is in giving that we receive,
it is in pardoning that we are par-
doned, and
it is in dying that we are born to
eternal life.

— St. Francis

As our understanding of our own suffering deepens, we become available at deeper levels to those we would care for. We are less likely to project suffering that does not exist or deny that which does. We're much more sensitive and alert to the nuances of human pain.

— Ram Dass

It is the darkest nights that prepare the greatest dawns.

— Sri Aurobindo

The power drive is given freest rein when it can appear under the cloak of objective and moral rectitude.

— Adolf Guggenbuhl - Craig

People must be given back the power to take charge of their own well-being — a power that is often taken away from them by systems of health care that tend to create dependence.

— Jack Schwarz

Leo was in the last stages of liver cancer. When he came to my office, he looked egg-yoke yellow. He reported that a hoped-for decision was not possible, that his ex-wife was already closing in for part of his estate, that his lawyer had said, "Don't worry, you're basically bankrupt," and that the pain was becoming intolerable. For some reason my spontaneous response was, "Other than that, how's your week been?" I was immediately concerned I had been inappropriate. However, Leo was laughing so hard I could hardly understand him as he said, "Thank goodness, someone still thinks I am alive! I am so tired of everyone treating everything so seriously."

—Ronna Fay Jevne, PhD.

It isn't easy to have cancer myself, but I don't believe that because you are told you have an illness that probably will be terminal, you should lose all hope. Why should you lose hope? If you lose hope, you might as well sit back in the rocking chair and say, "I'm gonna' die tomorrow." You have to have hope. I can't imagine living without hope.

— Pat, Patient

The fragrance of
the rose lingers
on the hand of the
giver.

— source unknown.

Not in Vain

If I can stop one heart
　　from breaking,
I shall not live in vain;
If I can ease one life the aching,
Or cool one pain,
Or help one fainting robin
Into his nest again,
I shall not live in vain.

— Emily Dickinson

"As I sat facing her, and she constantly contradicted me, I felt a desire to finally show her who was boss. I had a triumphant feeling that she did not realize how little she could do against my opposition." Such statements from social workers often describe very accurately the emotional situation. Quite frequently, the issue at stake appears to be not the welfare of the protected but the power of the protector.

— Adolf Guggenbuhl - Craig

I realize there's something I do before I start a session. I let myself know that I am enough. Not perfect. Perfect wouldn't be enough. But that I am human, and that is enough. There is nothing this [client] can say or do or feel that I can't feel in myself. I can be with him. I am enough.

— Rachel Naomi Remen, M.D.

Because of the authority often ascribed to professionals, you are in a powerful position to enhance or diminish hope. You become an important person in the patient's life, whether you want to be or not. Interaction with the patient is itself a treatment. Inherent in your interactions is the potential to do harm or to enhance healing. The question for all who are caring for someone who is ill — professionals included — is not whether or not to have a relationship with the patient, but what will the nature of the relationship be?

—Ronna Fay Jevne, PhD.

You heal a brother
by recognizing
his worth.

— From A Course in Miracles

To study the Way is to study
the Self.
To study the Self is to forget
the Self.
To forget the Self is to be
enlightened by all things.
To be enlightened by all things
is to remove the barrier
between Self and Other.

— Dogen Zenji

Unless we as healers are willing to confront our own pain and darkness, we can never be truly open to that joining of energy with our patients that is necessary for the fullest healing process to take place for both.

— Niravni Payne

I think, when I read of the
    poet's desire,
That a house by the side of the
road would be good;
But Service is found in its
tenderest form
When we walk with the crowd
in the road.

— Walter J. Gresham, 1886

The curriculum of service provides us with information about our strengths, and we discover how these contribute to genuinely help-full service. Each time we drop our masks and meet heart-to-heart, reassuring one another simply by the quality of our presence, we experience a profound bond which we intuitively understand is nourishing everyone.

— Ram Dass

Paracelsus believed that the good doctor's therapeutic success largely depends on his ability to inspire the patient with confidence and to mobilize his will to health. By the way, he also recommended chastity and fasting to heighten diagnostic sensitiveness and to intensify one's hypnotic power.

— Prince Charles of Wales

Give someone a fish and they're fed for a day.
Teach someone to fish and they're fed for a lifetime.

— source unknown

Touch is an integral part of nursing, yet its meaning can be difficult to articulate. It is used in a variety of ways to comfort, soothe, feel, appreciate, understand, respect, and heal. Its use as a vehicle for communication, however, remains unsurpassed, particularly in the discipline of nursing. No matter whether a patient is conscious or unconscious, young or old, ambulatory or immobile, black or white, literate or illiterate, nurses are able to effectively communicate through touch. In a simple touch, more love and understanding can be conveyed than could have been communicated with any amount or words.

— M. Patricia Donahue, RN.

Loving others is an expression of our love for God.

— Mother Teresa of Calcutta

There is in every true heart a
spark of heavenly fire,

which lies dormant
in the broad daylight of prosperity;

but which kindles up and beams
and blazes
in the dark hour of adversity.

— Anonymous Proverb

The intensity is not always comfortable, but I find strength in an awareness that when I'm with a patient, I can call on something greater than myself. You can call it God, Spirit, Energy, Consciousness, Love. I call it God. When I have that awareness, I am able to do the simple things that matter.

— Alice, Nurse and clinical coordinator

Judging from the severity of my withdrawal when I left nursing, I soon found out about a very real addiction to misery: I knew nothing about how to be joyful.

—Caryn Summers, R.N.

It is time for us to break free of our overly serious approach to life and laugh, have fun, cultivate frivolity, and joy. We {helpers} need to learn how to say "Yes!" — to having fun, to going on adventures, to attending spiritual retreats, to spontaneous outings, to developing our artistic talents, to listening to music, to reading enjoyable books, to soaking in bubble baths, to exercising regularly, to filling our homes with cut flowers and beauty and art.

— Carmen Renee Berry

To heal is to live one's life as a prayer, accepting our natural state of pure joy and happiness, peace and love, and extending that to all life.

— Gerald Jampolsky, M.D.

A Nurse's Prayer

When I falter, give me courage.
When I tire, renew my
strength.
When I weaken because I'm human,
Inspire me on to greater length.

If doctors and patients become
demanding,
and days are too short for all my duty,
Help me remember I chose to serve,
to do so with grace, and spiritual
beauty.

In humility Lord, I labor long hours —
and though I sometimes may fret;
My mission is mercy, abide with me,
that I may never forget.

— Source Unknown

If it's prison we're in, we right-eous helpers, what are we charged with? Breaking and enter-ing with the intention of doing good? Felonious assumption of personal responsibility? Selling water by the river? And what is our defense? Early conditioning? "They made me read Helper Rabbit every night until I was eight, Your Honor. In my house, the cry 'Help!' was an order, not a plea."

— Ram Dass

Being stuck in the past is just another form illusion can take. The message seems to be: Complete, with honesty, whatever is bothering you, and then...stop looking back.

— Jacquelyn Small

As people who are ministering to those facing life-and-death issues every day, we doctors are privileged to be in a position to benefit from the hard-won wisdom of our patients. The men and women — and children too — who have looked death in the face, are often those who know most about living. Their message is: 'I learned I was going to die and so I decided to live until I died.' They interpret their diagnosis not as a sentence but as a message to live. Their mortality is accepted, not seen as a verdict. How few of us know how to do that!

— Bernie Siegel, M.D.

*O*nly those who
dare, truly live.

— Ruth P. Freedman

I could be the perfect nurse — the nurse who skips her own lunch to feed the patient with meningitis, who works overtime and doesn't charge the hospital budget, who comes in early and works an extra shift to help out, who knows what it is like to be needed and who loves being needed, indeed, needs to be needed. I could be that nurse, the perfect nurse who is in control.

— Caryn Summers, R.N.

Being addicted to helping is so common, yet it is one of those problems seldom discussed. If I were addicted to drugs or alcohol, I'd have groups like Alcoholics Anonymous and substance abuse treatment programs to help me. If I were addicted to food or gambling or even sex, there would be people sharing my problem, to accept and help me break free. But there are no Messiah Anonymous groups waiting for us Messiahs. Why not? We are too busy pretending we have no problems, too busy focusing on everyone else's addictions, to face our own and to offer genuine help to each other.

— Carmen Renee Berry

Sad that so often [helping] imprisons us, that because of it we find ourselves accomplices to conditions of separateness and division — a world of nurses and patients, social workers and clients, spiritual teachers and seekers, people who know and people who don't. After all, if some of us are busy being helpers there must be others under continuous pressure to be helped.

— Ram Dass

Codependent Thought for the Day: "So many people to rescue, so little time."

— Jann Mitchell

If we become personally involved and experience feelings, we would lose our ability to help. We would become a hindrance to the healing process. In being professional we often have to be so callous and indifferent to feelings that we become like robots. I sometimes wonder if our motivation for doing this kind of work in the first place isn't related to our need to gain power over feelings of helplessness. The real tragedy is that we become so good at deluding ourselves that we lose touch with our own souls.

— Don, a Counselor

N

othing is needed in our lives more than healing, both for the patient and for the healer.

— Caryn Summers, R.N.

Hearts that have known pain meet in mutual recognition and trust. Such a meeting helps immeasurably.

— Ram Dass

Here, in a neonatal intensive care unit, you see incredible beauty and unbearable pain. And you have to figure out how to be with both.

— A Nurse

"I can do a score of things that can't be done," the Golux said. "I can find a thing I cannot see and see a thing I cannot find. The first is time, the second is a spot before my eyes. I can feel a thing I cannot touch and touch a thing I cannot feel. The first is sad and sorry, the second is your heart. What would you do without me? Say 'nothing.'"

"Nothing," said the Prince.

"Good. Then you're helpless and I'll help you...."

— James Thurber

We show lack of trust by trying to dominate and force the other into a mold, or by requiring guarantees as to the outcome, or even by "caring" too much.

— Milton Mayeroff

I know, you feel insecure, don't know what to say, don't know what to do. But please believe me, if you care, you can't go wrong. Just admit that you care. That is really for what we search. We may ask for whys and wherefores, but we don't really expect answers. Don't run away ... wait ... all I want to know is that there will be someone to hold my hand when I need it. I am afraid ... I have lots I wish we could talk about. It really would not take much more of your time... If only we could be honest, both admit of our fears, touch one another. If you really care, would you lose so much of your valuable professionalism if you even cried with me? Just person to person? Then it might not be so hard to die ... in a hospital ... with friends close by.

— student nurse who is dying,
to the medical staff

The physician who under-
stands the importance of
sitting at a bedside, even
though his presence may
actually be in the nature of a
placebo, is tending to a
prevalent and therefore,
quintessential need.

— Norman Cousins

People don't know what it's like to sit there with those bottles dangling. You're on chemo treatments twenty-one out of twenty-four hours a day. Your veins give out. They start talking about using the ones in your legs or cutting a hole in your chest. Your hair starts falling out. There is just too much happening to you. People don't understand what it feels like to eat soup and watch your hair fall in your bowl. That's really scary.

— Murray, Patient

We sometimes speak as if caring did not require knowledge, as if caring for someone, for example, were simply a matter of good intentions or warm regard. But in order to care I must understand the other's needs and I must be able to respond properly to them, and clearly good intentions do not guarantee this.

— Milton Mayeroff

You may be running so fast
to meet deadlines,
answering phone calls,
squeezing in one more client,
and feeling everyone else's
pain that you don't stop long
enough to feel your own pain.

— Carmen Renee Berry

W e need
heart-to-heart
resuscitation.

— Ram Dass

We have nothing to lose by a reexamination of fundamental assumptions of our models of health; on the contrary, we face the extraordinary possibility of fashioning a system that emphasizes life instead of death, and unity and oneness instead of fragmentation, darkness, and isolation.

— Larry Dossey, MD.

An attitude of not having anything further to learn is incompatible with caring.

— Milton Mayeroff

Disclosing and sharing some parts of our own lives is involved in forming a real connection. Patients need to feel they are in a real relationship — one where they give as well as receive. If "professionals" are unwilling to answer at least some personal questions, it is unlikely the necessary trust will happen. When a patient asks, "Do you have family?" they are not prying. It is a way of inquiring whether you are in a position to understand their feelings.

— Ronna Fay Jevne, PhD.

When one is a stranger to oneself, then one is estranged from others.. if one is out of touch with oneself, then one cannot touch others.

— Anne Morrow Lindbergh

Compassion and pity are very different. Whereas compassion reflects the yearning of the heart to merge and take on some of the suffering, pity is a controlled set of thoughts designed to assure separateness. Compassion is the spontaneous response of life; pity, the involuntary reflex of fear.

— Ram Dass

Each person faces a time of danger and a time of potential transformation. It's not for any of us to judge their response. It is for us to "be there" for them, not necessarily to "do" for them.

— Graeme, Psychologist

Two crucial requirements of the healing process are trust and honesty. By trust I mean that both the healer and the person to be healed have confidence that there is a power within the body that has the capacity to bring about healing when it is given the opportunity to do so. By honesty I mean the healer's willingness to be faithful and true to the spirit of the patient. These two qualities are the key strands in the golden thread that binds together all methods of healing.

— Emmet E. Miller, M.D.

Trust in the other to grow and in my own ability to care gives me courage to go into the unknown, but it is also true that without the courage to go into the unknown such trust would be impossible.

— Milton Mayeroff

Do not stand at my grave
and weep.

I am not there. I do not sleep.
I am a thousand winds that blow.
I am the diamond glints on snow.
I am the sunlight on ripened grain.
I am the gentle autumn's rain.

When you waken in the
morning's hush,
I am the swift uplifting rush
of quiet birds in circled flight.
I am the soft stars that shine
at night.

Do not stand at my grave and cry;
I am not there. I did not die.

— Source unknown

The pain of the world will sear and break our hearts because we can no longer keep them closed. We've seen too much now. To some degree or other, we have surrendered into service and are willing to pay the price of compassion.

But with it comes the joy of a single, caring act. With it comes the honor of participating in a generous process in which one rises each day and does what one can. With it comes the simple, singular grace of being an instrument of Love, in whatever form, to whatever end.

— Ram Dass

If you try to isolate against the feelings, you get hard. If you try not to be touched by the pain and suffering around you, you are not going to make it. It sounds contradictory. You have to be open to the pain and then you can deal with it. If you try to block it off, then you become cynical. It's a black hole not to care.

— Nola, Nurse and Nurse Educator

We are healed of
a suffering only
by experiencing it to
the full.

— Marcel Proust

*C*aring is the
*C*antithesis of
simply using the other
person to satisfy one's
own needs.

— Milton Mayeroff

The more you think of yourself as a "therapist", the more pressure there is on someone to be a "patient". The more you identify as a "philanthropist", the more compelled someone feels to be a "supplicant." The more you see yourself as a "helper," the more need for people to play the passive "helped." You're buying into, even juicing up, precisely what people who are suffering want to be rid of: limitation, dependency, helplessness, separateness. And that's happening largely as a result of self-image.

— Ram Dass

To detach means to give others the freedom to grow through their own mistakes and experiences. It is not feeling responsible for others, but rather allowing others to learn self-responsibility.

— Caryn Summers, R.N.

"The degree to which I can create relationships which facilitate the growth of others as separate persons is a measure of the growth I have achieved in myself.

— Carl R. Rogers.

Please Listen

When I ask you to listen to me
and you start giving advice,
you have not done what I asked
nor heard what I need.

When I ask you to listen to me
and you begin to tell me why I
shouldn't feel that way,
you are trampling on my feelings.

When I ask you to listen to me
and you feel you have to do something to solve my problems,
you have failed me — strange as
that may seem...

(cont.)

When you do something for me
that I can and need to do
for myself,
you contribute to me seeming fearful
and weak.

So, please listen and just hear me.

And if you want to talk, let's plan
for your turn,
and I promise I'll listen to you.

— Anonymous

Sometimes when we feel clumsy or inadequate in our efforts to care for an ailing family member, the healthiest way to respond is to laugh at our own imperfections. We human beings have an amazing capacity to be awkward, to say the wrong thing, or to mess up at the most inopportune moments. But if you can't laugh at your own guilt feelings, all you can do is cry.

— Leonard Felder, Ph.D.

There is a divine
plan of good at
work in my life. I will
let go and let it unfold.

— Ruth P. Freedman

When we look at the profound impact martyrs like Christ or Gandhi have had on the world, it is understandable that some people respond by glorifying martyrdom itself. At a more complex level of analysis, however, one need not conclude that their example requires the rest of us to be martyred. There are many different missions, many different paths. For Christ, dying freely for love's sake was a fulfillment of his life.

For another person, martyrdom might be an escape from the tough demands of life. The beginning of wisdom is being able to distinguish between transformative sacrifice and mere suffering caused because we are too cowardly or too unimaginative to think of a more joyous way to live.

— Carol S. Pearson

I slept and dreamt that life
was joy.
I awoke and saw that life
was service.
I acted and behold, service
was joy.

— Rabindranath Tagore

It is my personal belief that God wants us to spend less time asking, "Am I at fault for my loved one being ill?" and more time answering the question, "Now that a loved one is hurting, what can be done to help? What can I do to assist this person right now and to prevent suffering for others in the future?"

— Leonard Felder, Ph.D.

Life is tragic, but not necessarily serious. We are small people, here for a while. The sands will soon cover over our seemingly important enterprises. Let's do our best, respect each other, and hope that someone's passage is the better for our existence.

— Neil, Physician

Whenever we think of our-selves as doing something for someone else, we are in some way denying our own responsibility. Whatever we do is done because we choose to do it, and we make that choice because it is the one that satisfies us the most. Whatever we do for someone else we do because it fulfills a need we have.

— M. Scott Peck, M.D.

$\mathcal{J}$ have a clear choice
between life and death,
between reality and fantasy,
between health and sickness. $\mathcal{J}$
have to become responsible —
responsible for mistakes as
well as accomplishments.

— Eileen Mayhew

We do not increase our value when we make other people happy, gain people's trust, or provide them with the things they need. {Helpers} do not move up a notch on the 'worth' scale by giving to the poor, protecting the vulnerable, or rescuing those in crisis. The causes for which you fight may be worthy, but they do not increase your worth.

— Carmen Renee Berry

In our attempts to be more spiritual, we falsely believe that "yes" is a higher response than "no." Each is just as important as the other. In fact, if we are afraid of saying "no," than saying "yes" will have little power.

— Barry and Joyce Vissell

Some persons who came to
help us with the problems
of the refugees of Bangladesh
said that they had received
more than they gave to those
whom that had served.

— Mother Teresa of Calcutta

I shall not pass this way again
I shall pass
through this world but once.

Any good that I can do,
Or any kindness that I can show,
Let me not defer nor neglect it.

For I shall not pass this way again.

— source unknown

$\mathcal{T}$o love yourself is
to heal yourself.

— From A Course in Miracles

True selflessness is not the abandonment of self, but rather the surrender of selfish motives. The result of this surrender is self love, or self-esteem. We experience our preciousness and value and reach out from that centered place of love, serving authentically.

— Caryn Summers, R.N.

I've been chronically ill for twelve years. Stroke. Paralysis. That's what I'm dealing with now. I've gone to rehab program after rehab program. I may be one of the most rehabilitated people on the face of the earth. I should be President.

I've worked with a lot of people, and I've seen many types and attitudes. People try very hard to help me do my best on my own. They understand the importance of that self-sufficiency, and so do I. They're positive and optimistic. I admire them for their perseverance. My body is broken, but they still work very hard with it. They're very dedicated. I have nothing but respect for them.

But I must say this: I have never, ever, met someone who sees me as whole...

— Patient

Victimhood is a myth that only leads to powerlessness. If you are a counselor and perceive your client as a victim of anything, refer her to another counselor immediately! You can do no one any good unless you can guide them to their strengths and to the meaning behind their negative experiences.

— Jacquelyn Small

One of the challenges of taking good care of a loved one who needs you is to simultaneously bring some rays of hope into your physical environment. Make sure you open the curtains and let in some sunshine. Buy yourself some flowers every few days to add some color and brightness to your home. Have some good books, relaxing music, and tasty food available so you can unwind in comfort. Hire someone or ask a volunteer from a local service group to help clean your home thoroughly every so often. Make sure you take a long walk or get some exercise as frequently as possible.

— Leonard Felder, Ph.D.

Joy has no cost. It is your sacred right.

— From A Course in Miracles

The deaths get to me at times. I remember my dad telling me, over a breakfast of greasy fried eggs and logs of butter on the toast, "Everybody is not dying, no matter what you think. Go and walk along the sidewalk, look at the buds on the trees, and try to keep things in proper perspective."

— Diane, Nurse

I say we only fail if we are trying to keep people from being dead. Then we will inevitably fail, since life has a 100 percent mortality rate.

— Bernie Siegel, M.D.

One patient, when confronted
with a dismal future leading to
the grave, asked her doctor (who
made the prognosis), 'But what can
I do?' He replied, 'You only have
a hope and prayer.' She asked,
'How do I hope and pray?' And
he said 'I don't know, that's not my
line.'

— Bernie Siegel, M.D.

We shall never know all the good that a simple smile can do.

— Mother Teresa of Calcutta

The doctor I would want for myself or for anyone else I cared about would be one who understands that disease is more than just a clinical entity; it is an experience and a metaphor, with a message that must be listened to. Often the message will speak to us of our path and how we have strayed from it, so that our life is no longer a true expression of the inner self, or, as Larry LeShan would say, we are no longer singing our own song. Only by listening to that message can we mobilize all the healing powers that lie within, and that is what the doctor must help each patient to do.

— Bernie Siegel, M.D.

We have thousands of lepers. They are so brave, so admirable, disfigured as they are. Last Christmas I went to see them and said to them that they have God's care, that God loves them specially, that they are very dear to Him and their malady is not sin.

An old man who was completely disfigured came up to me and said: "Repeat that again; it does me good. I had always heard that no one loves us. It is wonderful to know that God loves us. Say it again."

— Mother Teresa of Calcutta

When one's all right, he's
    prone to spite
the Doctor's peaceful mission;
But when he's sick,
it's loud and quick
He bawls for a physician!

— Eugene Field, 1865

What are the changes which create a healing environment? They start with the introduction of laughter, music, love, forgiveness and acceptance, all coming after a release of resentment, conflict and despair. Every cell in the body is then involved in the healing process. When we laugh every cell laughs.

— Bernie Siegel, M.D.

I believe there is no disease whose treatment cannot be enhanced by a doctor who knows how to inspire and guide patients and so to bring into play the body's internal healers.

— Bernie Siegel, M.D.

Healing is a matter of time, but it is sometimes also a matter of opportunity.

—Hippocrates, 460-377 B.C.

I Never Knew a Night So Black

I never knew a night so black
  Light failed to follow on its
track.

I never knew a storm so gray,
It failed to have its clearing day.

I never knew such bleak despair,
That there was not a rift, some-
where.

I never knew an hour so drear,
Love could not fill it full of cheer.

— source unknown

The greatest healers do not participate in the myth of the All-Powerful. They sense their own limitations as surely as they know their strengths. They know, too, the necessity of illness in human life and its dynamic interrelatedness with health. For them the light and shadows are both essential ingredients of healthiness, and they do not attempt to ignore one in favor of the other.

— Larry Dossey, M.D.

Guilt is one of the most equal-opportunity employers, especially when it comes to family matters of illness and health. Different people express their guilt feelings in different ways — some keep them hidden inside while others are quite obvious about their feelings of remorse. However, you don't have to be Jewish, Catholic, Asian, or anything but human in order to worry that you're not doing enough for someone who needs so very much. Except for certain sociopaths, criminals, and narcissists who've lost their ability to feel concern for anyone but themselves, the rest of us have a tendency to feel guilty from time to time.

— Leonard Felder, Ph.D.

If I've been taught to feel guilty when I take time for myself, I then believe that I should be helping more, I ought to take on one more committee, I must help one more patient even though my shift is over, or I should help a family member even though I am tired. I must keep serving and smiling even though I'm exhausted and on the verge of tears.

— Caryn Summers, R.N.

Perhaps few things are more encouraging to another than to realize that his growth evokes admiration, a spontaneous delight or joy, in the one who cares for him. He experiences my admiration as assuring him that he is not alone and that I am really for him. His awareness of my delight in his efforts to grow has a way of recalling him to himself: I help him realize and appreciate what he has done. It is as if I said to him, "Look at yourself now, see what you did, see what you can do."

— Milton Mayeroff

Hope is basically a shared experience. When people share hopes, the illness experience is less lonely, for everyone. It is difficult to hope alone.

— Ronna Fay Jevne, PhD.

*T*he decision to be open is probably the most important single step toward healing.

— O. Carl Simonton

A patient becomes my favorite as soon as our relationship allows them to become authentic. They're authentic when they are themselves — be that eccentric or angry, curious or depressed, sad or joyful. I know then that we trust each other. They just about all become my favorite.

— Alice, Nurse

Examine me, O Lord, and try me.

— the Twenty-sixth Psalm

We can offer our own empathy, our own experience, our own understanding of how it feels when we suffer: the resistance, tension, fear, withdrawal, self-pity, doubt, the utter separateness. This compassion will guide our helping hand to appropriate gestures: a simple word of friendship to cut through the isolation; a gentle neck massage to ease the tension; a tender hug or touch to convey love; a meeting of the eyes for a moment beyond it all.

— Ram Dass

What is important to us is the individual. To get to love a person, there must be close contact. If we wait for the numbers, we will be lost in the numbers, and we will never be able to show that person the necessary love and respect. Every person is for me the only person in the world at that moment.

— Mother Teresa of Calcutta

We consider it vital that our medical staff have a practical, living experience of two basic laws:

1. The Golden Rule: Do to your patient as you would do to yourself.

2. The Second Commandment: Love your patient as yourself.

— Ernesto Contreras, M.D.

I do not try to help
the other grow in
order to actualize
myself, but by helping
the other grow I do
actualize myself.

— Milton Mayeroff

If You Want Happiness

If you want happiness for an
hour —take a nap.
If you want happiness for a day —
go fishing.
If you want happiness for a month
— get married.
If you want happiness for a year
—inherit a fortune.
If you want happiness for a lifetime
—help someone else.

— Chinese Proverb

$\mathcal{E}$very day is another chance to discover more about yourself — what are your strengths and limitations as a caregiver; what are you really like as a family member or friend; what are you learning about your own ability to express love, patience, and caring; and what are you discovering about your priorities in life?

— Leonard Felder, Ph.D.

Fortunately psychoanalysis is not the only way to resolve inner conflicts. Life itself still remains a very effective therapist.

— Karen Horney

Why not become trans-
formers of mankind,
rather than self-depleting reformers
who criticize and seek to correct?
A transformer creates the new
through that which already is, a
reformer seeks to destroy that
which is in hopes that something
better will take its place. The
reformer's work is ceaseless, never
ending, never satisfied. The work
of the transformer is always complete and perfect within itself; it is
always at peace as the energy
streams through it out into the world
to heal, transform, energize and
uplift. Allow yourself to be the
transformer — which you truly are.

— Alexis Edwards

Have the courage to act instead of react.

— Darlene Larson Jenks.

I never take care of crowds, only of a person. If I stopped to look at the crowds, I would never begin.

— Mother Teresa of Calcutta

Touch, as an act of understanding, can give ener-
gy, love, respect, and dignity to
those who are vulnerable and
whose lives are untrusted to
nurses... Touch truly unites the
head, the heart, and the hands
of the nurse to provide the
strong foundation for modern-
day nursing.

— M. Patricia Donahue, RN.

When I asked God what to do when confronted with a patient with a serious illness who I could help or God could heal, He said, "Render unto the doctor what is the doctor's and unto God what is God's."

— Bernie Siegel, M.D.

What is true healing? And what is the place of the healer within the healing process? In my eighty years, I seem to experiment with a whole range of answers to these vital questions. Through the process of 'discovering the healer,' with its leaps of understanding and moments of self-discovery, I have experienced the vital importance of a surrendered heart. When our primary motivation is to be totally available to the life process, any distinction between 'healer' and 'healee' disappears, and there is only one I AM.

— Frances Horn

Patience is not waiting passively for something to happen, but is a kind of participation with the other in which we give fully of ourselves. It is misleading to understand patience simply in terms of time, for we give the other space as well. By patiently listening to the distraught man, by being present for him, we give him space to think and feel. Perhaps, instead of speaking of space and time, it would be truer to say that the patient man gives the other room to live; he enlarges the other's living room, whereas the impatient man narrows it.

— Milton Mayeroff

It is nothing to hurl at one another — "Open to your pain!" — as if it didn't require great patience and discipline, a willingness to fail, fall, and try once more. The practice is not heartless, not rooted in any kind of denial of what's entailed. It is a practice of compassion for ourselves — the very same attentive listening and patient open-heartedness we would eagerly offer another.

— Ram Dass

As I think back on the times in my life when a special person was ailing or in need of care, I remember feeling scared. But I also recall having a deep sense of love and a strong sense of purpose. What you are doing to assist another human being is extremely worthwhile. Now if you can just remember to take good care of yourself, too, you'll do an even better job. Good luck!

— Leonard Felder, Ph.D.

May you seek
after treasures
of precious gold, and
find them within the
hearts of others.

— Mary Summer Rain

I have remained a surgeon for two reasons: One is that most people refuse this challenge and I can still help them, but more importantly I would like to combine my mechanical skills with your healing skills to achieve the greatest potential. If I can make all of this credible, we can accomplish the incredible.

— Bernie Siegel

The heart does speak most eloquently if we listen with our inner ear. Nursing reaches out to the hearts of others to assist as midwives in the birthing of new consciousness. Nurses have frequent opportunities to facilitate the transformation of the experience of discomfort and disease into one of growth, renewal and opportunity. Let the heart speak clearly, and it will touch the world around!

— Susanna Davis, R.N.

Teachers can become entrapped in their specialness, if being unique allows them no place to be ordinary, to cry ordinary tears over ordinary problems. The Teacher may have no safe place to "come clean," to share genuine vulnerability and acknowledge failings. Teachers can be surrounded by people and yet agonizingly alone. Teachers may be dismayed to find that no one is touching them.

— Carmen Renee Berry

Just like heavy rainfall clears the air and is followed by the sweet sounds of birds singing, so does a good cry bathe your insides with a healing release. Yet you might be saying, "I'm too busy to cry" or "I have to be strong — I can't let the tears come." But in fact we all need to cry at times like these. Even if you have great hopes that your loved one will recover soon and be well again, there's still a buildup of sadness that needs to come out.

— Leonard Felder, Ph.D.

No physician, in so far as he is a physician, considers his own good in what he prescribes, but the good of his patient; for the true physician is also a ruler having the human body as a subject, and is not a mere money-maker.

— Plato, 427-347 B.C.

There seems to be a movement today to reintroduce medical students to their patients as human beings, not diseases, and I think that movement will spread, because it will be successful for both patient and doctor. If nothing else, today's consumer-conscious patients will pass the word among themselves, and the doctors who have gotten the message will get their business.

— Bernie Siegel, M.D.

"Did I help?" "Did it work?" "What did he feel?" "Why did she say that?" "What was really going on this morning?" "What if?... What if...?' "Try this.... no, try that." "If only..." And probably heaviest of all: "Was it really for the best? How do I know? How can I be sure? God, it's somebody's life!"

— Ram Dass

Identifying what you need and want may be more difficult than you imagine. By getting caught up in meeting the needs of others and giving them what they seem to want, you probably have spent little time listening to yourself.

— Carmen Renee Berry

I came to nursing without my own thinking (using research or others' ideas as my own), feeling ashamed of thoughts I had about healing, and fearful, believing I didn't have the right to speak up or out. Unaware of my neediness, I was able to use the theories of others and take care of others to shore myself up. I excelled, and my colleagues fed me the definition of myself that I created for them. I never felt full.

— David Willard

Many helpers, when they themselves are suffering, are incapable of accepting support, or at least receiving it easily. Yet they may be impatient with those they're working with for not accepting aid or counsel readily enough. Chances are, if you can't accept help, you can't really give it.

— Ram Dass

What we grew
up with, we
learned; what we
learned, we practiced;
and what we prac-
ticed, we became.

— Earnie Larsen

If you want to help a person — including yourself — who tends to give until it hurts, you need to take into account some deep-seated reasons why most caregivers can't stop giving, even when they become ill themselves. Ignoring these underlying psychological factors is like trying to pull a tree out of the ground without taking into account the extensive roots that keep the tree firmly in place.

— Leonard Felder, Ph.D.

When your negligence has resulted in someone's death, I can't describe the amount of guilt you feel. And then a moment comes when you move from utter humiliation to simple humility. It's your fault, but also somehow it isn't. We live lives where such things happen. And in that moment you begin to forgive yourself. You don't deny what you've done. You pass through it, it rips you up, and you come out the other end — with a new possibility that comes from that humility and self-forgiveness.

— Ram Dass

*C*ourage is the price that life exacts for peace.

— Amelia Earhart

Life is either a
daring adventure
or nothing.

— Helen Keller

When the deepest part of you becomes engaged in what you are doing, when your activities and actions become gratifying and purposeful, when what you do serves both yourself and others, when you do not tire within but seek the sweet satisfaction of your life and your work, you are doing what you were meant to be doing.

— Gary Zukav

We may assume people are suffering in ways that they aren't... We project discomfort onto people about their helplessness which doesn't necessarily exist, or we fail to see the character of the suffering that really is there. ... But more significant still are our past experiences facing our own suffering. Here is the next critical issue we need to engage — one that any of us who seeks to help another must confront sooner or later.

— Ram Dass

If people don't understand, they say the wrong thing. One of the wrong things to say is that you understand when you really don't.

— Joan, Patient

The impulse to do all we can to relieve one another's pain is the automatic response of our native compassion. But the experience of suffering — in ourselves and in others — triggers off complicated reactions. To investigate these is itself an act of compassion, an essential step toward becoming more effective instruments of mutual support and healing. How then do we respond to the pain we see around us? And, once we have investigated this response, how do we respond to our own afflictions?

— Ram Dass

The weariest night, the longest day, sooner or later must perforce come to an end.

— Baroness Orczy

When we learn both to take and to give, we can move into a flow of giving and receiving that is love's essence — reciprocity. In this way, the flow of energy does not go just one way, but both. I give to you and you to me and we both fully receive the energy. Christ said to "love your neighbor as yourself." Sacrifice, however, has been misinterpreted as loving your neighbor instead of yourself.

— Carol S. Pearson

In order to spread joy, it is necessary to have joy in one's family. Peace and war begin in the home. If we really want peace in the world, let us first love one another, in the family.

— Mother Teresa of Calcutta

For many, the ability to aid others can provide a needed sense of power or respectability. Maybe some of us help out as a way of compensating for a deeper sense of helplessness; we don't have to face our own quite so much when we're busy treating someone else's. Or maybe we're just plain lonely. Intimacy is what we're looking for, and it's often there to be found in a helping relationship.

— Ram Dass

Counselors are looked up to as people with answers — and are certainly not supposed to be people with problems.

Consequently, it may be difficult to find a place where the Counselor can be honest about inner struggles. Where does the pastor go to grapple with the affair he is having? Whom does the social worker confide in when she loses control and batters her child? Where do we go with our own inner pain?

— Carmen Renee Berry

In the treatment process, something happens to the clinician as well as to the patient (e.g., fear, distancing, anger, frustration, joy, satisfaction, etc..). Frequently, {there occur} defensive maneuvers on the part of the clinician to avoid confronting the emotions and memories which the patient evokes... in the clinician. In shutting out a part of the patient, we also close off access to an important part of ourselves. We can grow emotionally (if painfully) with our patients... if we can see beyond surgical 'repair,' patient 'compliance,' or drug 'efficacy.' Not that these latter are unimportant; but what whole are they a part of? What happens to us is as important as what happens to our patients.

— Howard F. Stein

Often what's happening is that "we gotta" get rid of someone's pain because it's hurting us too much.

— Ram Dass

To keep a lamp
burning we have
to keep putting oil in it.

— source unknown

For those nurses and doctors who are working in the hospital, I suggest going down to the chapel and sitting there quietly, several times during the day. This accomplishes many things. Among others, it changes the way you relate to the people you meet there as you deal with them later on: If you meditate or pray together with an x-ray technician, it is highly unlikely that you will berate that technician when you work together. So you change and relationships change.

— Bernie Siegel, M.D.

Pity is another way we keep suffering at arm's length. We may let in a little of someone's pain, but never enough to threaten our own self-control. We may feel a little moved to respond to the suffering — we'd feel guilty or uncomfortable if we didn't — but we'd like to get it all over with as soon as possible and get on with our own affairs.

— Ram Dass

Authentic service can be seen in the nurse who has nurtured herself, the healer who has been healed. It is the service we hear when the nurse can speak from her heart to the patient these simple and humble words, "I am here. Let's heal together. "

— Caryn Summers, R.N.

The longest journey is the journey inward, for he who has chosen his destiny has started upon his quest for the source of his being.

— Dag Hammarsjkold

If we are willing to examine the agitation of our own minds and look just beyond it, we quite readily find entry into rooms that hold surprising possibilities: a greater inner calm, sharper concentration, deeper intuitive understanding, and an enhanced ability to hear one another's heart. Such an inquiry turns out to be critical in the work of helping others.

— Ram Dass

Illness is the great equalizer. There is no immunity by virtue of rank or privilege. Each of us is only a diagnosis away from being subject to the artificial separations between patients and the rest of the world. Each of us could be asked to wear the unbecoming hospital gown, to wear the wrist band for identification, to share a room with a stranger, to undergo invasion after invasion, to tolerate repeated, unintended indignities in the pursuit of recovery. Each of us could be the person who is left uninvited to the party, unnoticed in the flurry of "normal" activities. Each of us could be the person that someone else thinks is dying. Each of us is potentially "the Patient."

— Ronna Fay Jevne, PhD.

The healed Healer
is more powerful
than ever the innocent.

— Caryn Summers, R.N.

INDEX TO TOPICS

267

INDEX TO AUTHORS

REFERENCES

Grateful acknowledgement is given to the original authors and to the publishers of these works, even where the passages are anonymous. Every attempt has been made to identify the sources, and where the source is unknown, this author gladly invites information which will appear in future editions of this book, provided written notification is received.

Berry, Carmen Renee. *When Helping You Is Hurting Me: Escaping the Messiah Trap.* Harper & Row. Copyright C. Berry, 1988.

Carlson, Richard, and Shield, Benjamin. *Healers on Healing.* Jeremy P. Tarcher. California. Copyright Carlson and Shield, 1989.

Church, Dawson & Sheer, Alan. *The Heart of the Healer.* New York. Copyright Aslan Publishers, 1987.

Donahue, Patricia M. PhD., RN. *Nursing: The Finest Art. Master Prints.* C.V. Mosby Co. Miss. Copyright C,V. Mosby Company, 1989.

Felder, Leonard. Ph.D. *When a Loved One is Ill: How to Take Better Care of Your Loved One, Your Family, and Yourself.* Penguin Books. New York. Copyright L Felder, 1991.

Fletcher, Douglas, R.N. Editor & Publisher. *The Journal of Nursing Jocularity.* Copyright D Fletcher, 1992.
Gorree, Georges and Barbier, Jean. *The Love of Christ: Spiritual Counsels from Mother Teresa of Calcutta.* New York. Copyright Harper & Row, 1982.

Guggenbuhl-Craig, Adolf. *Power in the Helping Professions*. Spring Publications, Dallas TX. Copyright Guggenbuhl-Craig, 1971.

Houston, Jean. *The Search for The Beloved*. Jeremy P. Tarcher, Inc. Los Angeles. Copyright J. Houston, 1987.

Jevne, Ronna Fay. Ph.D. *It All Begins with Hope. Patients, Caregivers & the Bereaved Speak Out*. San Diego, CA. LuraMedia. Copyright LuraMedia, Inc., 1991.

King, Laurel. *Women of Power*. Celestial Arts, California. 1989.

Kubler-Ross, Elizabeth. *Death: The Final Stage of Growth*. Prentice-Hall, Inc., Englewood Cliffs, N.J., Copyright E. Kubler-Ross, 1975.

Larry Dossey, MD., *Space, Time and Medicine*, Shambhala Publications, Boston, 1982.

Lewis, Richard. *Miracles: Poems by Children of the English-speaking World*. Simon and Schuster. Copyright R. Lewis, 1964.

Mayeroff, Milton. *On Caring*. Harper & Row, New York. Copyright Milton Mayeroff, 1971.

Miller, Alice. "Violence: Alice Miller's Impact on Psychotherapy," *The Common Boundary*, Vol. 5, Issue 3, May/June 1987.
Mitchell, Jann. *Codependent for Sure!* Andrews and McMeel. Copyright Parkside Publishing Corp., 1992.

Pearson, Carol S. *The Hero Within: Six Archetypes We Live By*. Harper & Row. Copyright Carol Pearson, 1986.

Peck, M. Scott. *The Road Less Traveled*. Simon and Schuster. 1978. Copyright 1978 by M. Scott Peck, M.D. Reprinted by permission of Simon & Schuster, Inc.

Ram Dass & Gorman, Paul. *How Can I Help?* New York. Alfred A. Knoff. Copyright Alfred A Knoff, 1985.

Schaef, Anne Wilson. Excerpted from *Women of Power*. Celestial Arts, California. Copyright 1989 by Laurel King. Reprinted by permission of Celestial Arts, P.O. Box 7327, Berkeley, CA 94707.

Siegel, Bernie S. M.D. *Peace, Love and Healing*. New York. Harper & Row. Copyright Bernie Siegel, 1989.

Small, Jacquelyn. *Transformers: The Therapists of the Future*. DeVorss & Company, Marina del Ray, Calif. Copyright J. Small, 1982.

Snow, Candace and Willard, David, R.N. *I'm Dying to Take Care of You: Nurses & Codependence, Breaking the Cycles*. Professional Counselor Books. WA. Copyright Snow and Willard, 1989.

Summers, Caryn Lea. R.N. *Circle of Health: Recovery Through the Medicine Wheel*. The Crossing Press. Freedom Ca. Copyright C. Summers, 1991.
Summers, Caryn. *Caregiver, Caretaker: From Dysfunctional to Authentic Service in Nursing*. Mt. Shasta. Commune-A-Key Publishing. Copyright C. Summers, 1992.

Thurber, James. *The 13 Clocks*. Simon & Schuster. NY. 1950.

Vissell Barry M.D. and Vissell, Joyce, R.N., M.S. *Risk to be Healed*. Copyright Ramira Publishing, 1989.

Zukav, Gary. *The Seat of the Soul*. Simon & Schuster. Copyright G. Zukav, 1989.

Many of the quotations from patients and individual helpers were taken from *How Can I Help?* or from *It All Begins With Hope*. Others were taken from interviews conducted by the author of this text.

ABOUT THE AUTHOR

Caryn Summers has worked within the nursing profession since 1978. She is currently a writer and speaker, presenting workshops for nurses and other helping professionals on topics of codependency, chemical dependency, recovery, and authentic service.

Caryn works with the California Board of Registered Nurses' Diversion Program, providing assessment and intervention for chemically impaired nurses in Northern California. She facilitates nurse support groups and provides private consultation to hospitals, employee assistance programs, and nursing staffs.

In her first book, *Circle of Health: Recovery through the Medicine Wheel*, Caryn provides creative tools for healing substance addictions or dysfunctional behavior patterns. This workbook utilizes symbols, Native American traditions, mythology, Jungian theory, and psychosynthesis. Caryn believes that the recovery, or healing, process can be imaginative and exciting, and facilitates Circle workshops for the audience who is interested in creative recovery.

In her second book, *Caregiver, Caretaker: From Dysfunctional to Authentic Service in Nursing*, Caryn addresses the motives behind dysfunctional service, or caretaking — the need to be needed, guilt, control, low self-esteem, and shame, as well as the motives for authentic service, or caregiving — compassion and self-growth. The book explains addictions, codependency, post-traumatic stress disorder, and institutional cobehavior using true stories and discussions. Written with safety, dignity, and respect, Caryn offers solutions for people working in an essential profession.

Founder of Commune-A-Key Publishing and Seminars, Caryn offers a unique blend of education, nurturing, fun, and adventure to professionals who attend her workshops.

Photo by Eric Poppke

ORDER FORM

Need copies for your friend? You may find books published by Commune-A-Key at your local bookstore, or you may order directly.

Inspirations for Caregivers, edited by Caryn Summers, R.N. A collection of uplifting and thought-provoking statements by well-known caregivers that praise, support and question the caregivers of the world about the motives and rewards for giving care to others.

Inspirations for Caregivers: Music and Words. Some of the best quotes from *Inspirations for Caregivers* with original piano music by Douglas York.

Circle of Health: Recovery Through the Medicine Wheel, by Caryn Summers, R.N. "Recovery means the regaining of self. This workbook combines art, mythology, symbols, Native American tradition and psychology with the tools practiced in many twelve-step recovery programs."

Caregiver, Caretaker: From Dysfunctional to Authentic Service in Nursing, by Caryn Summers, R.N. Essential reading for helpers who tend to care for others before caring for themselves. "This lucid, gripping book sounds a loud warning far beyond the confines of the nursing profession. It is a powerful message for all helping and healing professions."

Mail this form with your check or money order payable to:

Commune-A-Key Publishing
P O Box 507
Mt. Shasta, CA 96067

Title	Quantity	Price	Total
Inspirations for Caregivers	_____	$ 8.95 each	_____
Inspirations: Music & Words	_____	$10.95 each	_____
Caregiver, Caretaker	_____	$16.95 each	_____
Circle of Health	_____	$12.95 each	_____

Shipping and handling: $3.00 first book, $1.25 each additional _____

Total $ enclosed _____

_____
Name

_____
Address

_____   _____   _____
City   State   Zip

_____
Phone

☐ Please send me information on other products and seminars.

WHAT OTHERS ARE SAYING ABOUT THIS BOOK

"Finally, a book of inspiration for those who work so hard at inspiring others. Thank you for so many words of wisdom!"

—David Norris, Nurse Entrepreneur

"The title *Inspirations for Caregivers* is most appropriate: This is a most inspirational book! It is touching, insightful, caring, and heart-felt as well. A rare gift for caregivers."

—Dr. Margaret Hatcher, Associate
Executive Director for Excellence in
Education, Northern Arizona
University, Flagstaff, AZ.

"This book will inspire caregivers to recognize the gift of healing they each give as they lovingly touch those whom they serve. What a gift! What a book!

—Charlotte McGuire, RNC, MA,
Founder of the American Holistic
Nurses Association; Co-founder of
Southwest Institute for Women's
Healing Journeys